WINNING YOUR DIVORCE

The Top 10 Mistakes Men Make and How to <u>Avoid</u> Them.

Joseph F. Emmerth

Joseph F. Emmerth

WINNING YOUR DIVORCE:

The Top Ten Mistakes Men Make, And How to <u>Avoid</u> Them.

Copyright © 2017 by Joseph F. Emmerth

Cover Design by C5 Designs

Edited by Michelle Wulf

Author photographs by REP3

For information about special discounts for bulk purchases, please contact the Author, at jemmerth@gmail.com. Please put "Bulk Purchase" in the subject line of the email.

CONTENTS

INTRODUCTION

Most men try to torpedo their best interests during a divorce. In fact, most men tend to be absolute idiots during the process. It doesn't matter if they are CEOs, doctors, lawyers, scientists, professional athletes, captains of industry, or small business owners. Once the divorce starts, every skill and ability that got them where they are today goes straight out the window in favor of ill-conceived and in many cases, adolescent behavior. This leads directly to escalating hostility between divorcing spouses, an increased length of the process, an undermining their own goals, and a huge increase in the cost of the divorce.

But it doesn't have to be that way. This book was written to help men avoid the most common mistakes that they make during a divorce. This book provides a "roadmap" of potholes, bumps and ditches a divorcing man can easily avoid. By following the advice on how to avoid these pitfalls during a divorce, men can shorten the length of their divorce, save a ton of money on attorney's fees, and greatly reduce the stress and emotional turmoil.

I've been a divorce lawyer for over a decade, and have helped hundreds of men (and women) navigate the rough waters that accompany the end of a marriage. I've seen men make the same mistakes time and time again, completely sabotaging their own divorce. I've been voted a SuperLawyer by my peers and have received the Avvo Client's Choice Award by the clients whose divorces I've helped resolve. In addition to occupying various leadership positions in both the Illinois State Bar Association and also local bar associations, I'm a frequent presenter at continuing legal education seminars and other events. But before all of that, and before I chose to focus my time and energy on helping divorcing couples, I was a counselor. My time providing therapy to individuals gave me insights that have only served to increase and focus my effectiveness as a divorce lawyer.

Men who are struggling with the process, men who are angry, men who feel like just shutting down, men who want to punish their spouse, and men who just don't know what to do will all benefit from this book. You will experience a much more successful divorce if you can avoid the traps described in each chapter. "I wish I had known these things ahead of time", "I didn't know that doing some of these things would make things worse" and, "Thank God you told me to avoid that, because I was about to do it" are all comments I frequently hear after going over these issues with divorcing men.

If you follow the advice in this book, your divorce will be much less stressful, will be over much quicker, and will be much less expensive. Who doesn't want that? You should also realize that, even if you're in the middle of a divorce, and even if you've made some of the mistakes described in this book, IT'S NOT TOO LATE! If you are making some of these mistakes, simply stopping the behaviors or changing your approach will result in a more positive outcome. In fact, by changing or stopping some of these things during a divorce, it often sends a message to the other side that you have decided to finish the process in a more efficient, respectful and mature manner. This also shortens the length and decreases the cost of the divorce. So, don't hesitate to implement the advice in the following chapters. Don't throw your hands up in the air in hopelessness because you've made a few missteps. Correct them now!

Don't be the man that shoots himself in the foot during the divorce process. Don't cut off your nose to spite your face. Don't be the guy intent on ruining his own life. Be the man who actively works towards his goals. Be the man who takes control of life and resolves problems efficiently and without ramping up unnecessary stress. Be the kind of person other men look at and say, "I wish my divorce had gone as smoothly as his did."

Read this book now and avoid the mistakes described in each chapter. If you've already made some, then correct them. Each chapter will highlight an error to avoid or correct, and discuss exactly how to do so. Take control of your life, and look forward to accomplishing more of your goals. By creating this book, I've helped accomplish one of my primary goals: to help unhappy men become happy again. If you follow the advice in this book, in short order you will be happy again, too.

JOSEPH F. EMMERTH

Joseph F. Emmerth

For Joe and Brenda, who modelled what a loving marriage really looks like.

MISTAKE #1:
MOVING OUT OF THE MARITAL RESIDENCE

This is one of the most common mistakes that divorcing men make. Often, when men come in for a consultation, or just to seek advice about how to plan for a divorce, they've already taken steps to leave the marital residence. Make no mistake, in three-quarters of divorce cases this makes the case much more difficult to resolve. There are many reasons for this, and we're going to explore them here. Some of them might seem counterintuitive, but once you hear the rationale behind them they will make sense. Moving out of the marital house isn't an insurmountable mistake, but it can turn an even battle into an uphill one.

I sympathize with you guys. Believe me, I know she's driving you crazy. All the little gestures, quirky idiosyncrasies, and endearing habits that you've grown to recognize and cherish over the years have now turned into the most irritating things you have to deal with on a daily basis. The mere sight of her is enough to ruin your day. She has had the same amount of years to figure out exactly how to drive you over the edge. She knows all the buttons to push to set you on edge, and won't hesitate to use them. She will accentuate and embellish the behaviors that drive you insane. If she knows that leaving dirty dishes out irritates you, she will cook a Thanksgiving dinner and leave everything laying around. If she knows you like to save energy, she will turn on every light in the house. If she knows you like it on the chilly side, she will crank that heat up to 90°, just to piss you off. Your significant other has actually been taking a Masters-level class on <u>you</u> for the entirety of your relationship. She didn't realize it until things went south, but she has a PhD in getting under your skin, and she has just figured out how to apply that degree.

Of course, this drives you absolutely insane. Every single little thing is magnified a thousand times once your relationship starts to sour. Things you once tolerated will now whip you into a frenzy, and things that you put up with just to get along have now turned into things that you simply can't endure. I get it. But that doesn't mean you should leave the marital residence. You're now engaged in a battle. But in this battle, the weapons are behaviors, and they can be defended against just like any weapon can be defended against. This will require a high degree of determination and a measure of self-control that you haven't had to exercise until now. For some men, achieving a Zen-like state where nothing bothers them and every subtle provocation and deliberate irritation rolls off their back like water off a duck.

Most men aren't like that, and I don't expect you to be. However, there are some steps you can take to minimize your irritation. Staying out of the house more often than usual is one way to combat her strategy. Picking a certain room in the house and spending most of your time there free from her irritating attempts at provoking you is another. And then of course, there is always the option of fighting back. However, this usually tends to escalate things and I wouldn't recommend it. No one wins in a "War of the Roses" scenario. Just bear in mind that the level of success she has in pushing you over the edge is directly tied to your ability to control yourself. Exercise discipline and you can endure this.

Perhaps you're worried about the overall situation in the residence deteriorating quickly. Perhaps you think that these little irritating gestures and not-so-subtle provocations are merely preludes to something more serious. Maybe you think she's going to do something extreme like start throwing stuff out on the lawn, or deliberately provoking you into a physical fight. These are all legitimate concerns, and the purpose of this book is not to minimize the real risks that some people face when dealing with an erratic and unpredictable spouse under extreme stress. However, unless you have a clear indication that things are about to escalate into violence on her part, don't move out of the marital residence. There's a very good reason for this. As miserable as you might be, she is just as miserable. Both of you are going through an extremely stressful situation. You don't like each other, you don't want to be around each other, and you certainly don't want to see each other's face all the time. When things get tough and it seems like you just can't endure another minute in there, take a step back and realize that it's just as tough and just as hard for her to endure as it is for you, regardless of her antics or the things that she's trying to make you do. This is also when you should realize an important point regarding the marital home: by moving out, you will be giving her what she wants. She'll still wake up in her bed. She'll get to use her bathroom. She'll take a shower with her bath gel and dry off with her towels. She'll brush her teeth with her toothbrush and her toothpaste. She'll put on her makeup while she looks into her mirror. She'll walk downstairs to her kitchen, and make her breakfast with her appliances. She'll eat it with her fork and her plate. She'll open her closet and pick an outfit from among her clothes. Then she'll go out and get in her car and go about her daily life...without having to deal with you at all. By leaving the marital residence, you've given her a glimpse of her ultimate goal, a life lived just how she wants without any interference from you. She has all her stuff and gets to do whatever she wants, but she doesn't have to deal with you. It's like she has already won!

This usually has the effect of slowing down the divorce to a crawl. She now has no incentive to do anything. She has the status quo, but without you. Her stress level immediately goes down and she doesn't have the daily irritation of having to see your face. She's not going to be pressured into a settlement she doesn't want to sign, nor is she going to make decisions based on how to proceed efficiently and smoothly towards concluding this process, simply because she doesn't have to. Her day-to-day life and her ability to get through this period of time at her leisure (and on her timetable) has made the battle much easier for her, now that you've left the house.

For those of you who have children, leaving the marital residence has even sadder implications. Unless you're taking the children with you or unless there is already a parenting plan of some sort in place, by leaving the marital residence you have almost guaranteed that you are not going to be seeing your children as much. After all, you're not there. You won't be getting them up in the morning, won't be getting them ready for school, won't will be making their breakfast, and won't be taking them to school or other places. You've cut yourself out of the equation. She might have been more agreeable to working out a parenting schedule while she had the stress and the constant irritation of having to discuss it with you all the time, but now that you're gone she might no longer have any incentive to come to the table in good faith and work out a parenting time schedule that benefits you or the children. For those of you that have children, this is the most important reason you shouldn't voluntarily leave the marital residence. By deciding to leave, you're not just getting away from her. You're deliberately placing yourself into a scenario where your children won't have a father around on a regular basis. That alone should give you pause.

Another unintended side effect of leaving the marital residence is that sometimes it sends the wrong impression to the judge. It shouldn't matter, but sometimes it does, much like many things in life. If the issue of who gets the house is one of the items you're dealing with in your divorce process, the fact that you voluntarily left it might very well be the tiebreaker in the judge's eyes if your case winds up going to trial, or if the judge must make a decision. If your wife has a particularly cunning attorney they might try to use this against you in other ways, such as suggesting that you really weren't that interested in the residence anyway, or even more insidiously, that you really weren't interested in seeing your children that much. After all, if the children were your number one priority why would you ever leave them? Judges are people too, and while the vast majority of them do very, very good work, just like you and I they are occasionally swayed by things they shouldn't be and make decisions based on gut impressions rather than the law. Don't give them the opportunity to do so.

As a practical matter, there are other very valid reasons why you shouldn't leave the marital residence. If you leave, obviously, you'll have to find somewhere else to live. Unless you have a brother-in-law with a moldy basement, or a sympathetic parent to welcome you back to your nautical-themed bedroom in the attic, you'll have to pay to stay somewhere. In essence, you just increased your expenses, or perhaps even doubled them. Finances are one of the most frequent sources of tension in any marriage, and they are very often one of the main factors leading to a divorce. So, by drastically increasing your expenses, you might unintentionally wind up throwing fuel on an already raging fire. If your spouse doesn't work, or if you have children, there will undoubtedly come a time in the process where they ask the court to order you to pay support. If you have committed yourself or invested in another place to stay, you may find yourself below the poverty line once you must start giving money to your spouse and children. That $2,500 a month condo in a prime downtown location might not seem that enticing once you crunch the numbers and realize you have $25 a week to spend on food, after paying support.

Additionally, there is another fiscal concept that comes into play when you leave the marital residence. If your divorce is one where you are most likely going to have to pay your spouse support, consider this: many courts won't award support to a spouse if everyone is still living under the same roof. The court often reasons that if the parties are maintaining the status quo and the bills are being paid, then no one needs to be giving anybody money on a monthly basis. However, once you leave the marital residence the court may decide that there are now two separate households. And if your wife is unemployed, has never worked, or simply makes far less than you do, the court might very well award her support. At this point you quickly come to the realization that you screwed up, not once, but twice. Not only have you removed her number one source of stress and given her what she wants, you now must finance her lifestyle. So, she finds herself in an optimal position: she gets to live essentially the same life she had, which you pay for, but without you being around.

Only in America! Those seven-dollar dessert drinks at Starbucks? Those imported Belgian chocolates? Those once a week massages, those tennis lessons, those expensive shoes? Not a problem! So now, while she's meeting up with friends three times a week for cosmopolitans and chocolate martinis, you're left deciding which item off the dollar value menu you want for dinner.

The philosophical and strategic reasons for staying in the marital house are pretty simple. You want to keep the pressure on her to ensure that she is just as motivated and invested to move the divorce process along as you are. Also, it's better to know what she's up to than not know what she's up to. There's a lot of intelligence that can be gleaned just from observing your spouse closely. When they go to see their lawyer, what they say to you in response to different topics, what they talk to their friends about, what they say to the children, what things you say that irritate them and what things you say that don't, these can all be valuable when formulating your strategy during the divorce.

Fair warning, sometimes the intelligence that you glean from staying in the marital house won't be intelligence that you want to hear, particularly in cases of infidelity. However, if your wife is stepping out with someone else or if she has already moved on emotionally it's probably better for you to know than to find out later from someone else. While it's tempting to try and identify the particular individual she has replaced you with, that's not really the point. The point is that it's a lot harder for her to hide an affair from you if you're there in the house, and this may have several ramifications depending upon the laws of your state. In some states, if your wife already has a boyfriend, it can affect custody proceedings. If she intends to move in with this boyfriend after the marriage, it can very often impact whether or not she receives spousal support from you. Some states even still regard adultery as a crime. So, it's far better for you to know if your spouse is cheating from the get-go. It's far easier for you to find it out if you remain in the marital residence.

MISTAKE #2:
CREATING NEW ASSETS

Mistake number two sometimes dovetails with mistake number one. Let's say you've ignored the advice in the previous chapter and you're planning to move out of the marital residence, or you have already moved out. Now, there may be some very valid reasons why you had to leave the marital residence. Perhaps the residence was your spouse's premarital house and you simply had to go. Maybe the divorce has been going on for little bit and they filed a motion for exclusive possession of the residence, which was granted. Or perhaps things degenerated to the point where physical violence occurred, and an order of protection or domestic violence charge mandates that you leave the residence. These situations result in you having to make some decisions, decisions that become much more difficult when considering your marital status and the divorce process.

Most personal finance articles and financial planners will tell you that it's always preferable to buy a residence than to rent, so that you may begin accumulating equity and/or improving your credit score. However, this advice can backfire if you are married, and particularly if you are going through a divorce. In most states, any assets or debts acquired during the marriage are going to be considered marital property by the courts, regardless of whose name appears on the asset or debt. This can pose some tricky choices for you. If you purchase a new home or a condo after leaving the marital residence, that new house or condo will most likely be considered marital property. Congratulations, you've now created yet another asset that must be divided between the two of you. And, in certain circumstances, if you had other reasonable places to stay temporarily, a court might even find that the funds you have used for a down payment could be considered dissipation. Dissipation is a legal term, sometimes called by other names, depending upon the state in which you live, which essentially states that a portion of any funds used for nonmarital purposes during a divorce may be subject to reimbursement to the other spouse. This clearly complicates things for you if you are looking to purchase a new place to live. Often, it's much simpler and much easier to simply bite the bullet and rent or lease an apartment until the divorce is over.

Another problem with purchasing a new residence is that you will undoubtedly want to furnish said residence. Unless you've purchased a studio condo, you will most likely spend thousands of dollars (sometimes tens of thousands of dollars) buying furniture, appliances and technology for the residence. Even if the court doesn't penalize you for using marital funds to purchase a new residence, they will certainly not look favorably upon you utilizing further marital resources to furnish a new residence. Be very careful when considering the ramifications and consequences of purchasing a new residence during a divorce. It's also wise to consider your cash flow when making this type of decision. Even if you've weighed the pros and cons and decided to purchase a residence anyway, and even if you're able to get by without spending much money to furnish it, don't forget the other expenses involved with owning a house. You're going to have insurance premiums, utilities, property taxes, and maybe even HOA fees. These are on top of the same expenses that must be paid on the residence you just left. Do not underestimate the sometimes crushing expense of having to maintain two households instead of one. It's not always the purchase itself that leads to problems financially.

There are two exceptions to this general principle. First, your spouse may want you out of the house so badly that she agrees to let you take an advance against your share of the marital estate to put a down payment on a new piece of property. If you're willing to do this, and you don't foresee any of the pitfalls in chapter one coming into play, then perhaps this is an option you are willing to accept. This means she is agreeing that, whatever the eventual division of assets and debts, the money you are taking out now for the down payment will simply come out of your share at the end. It is a simple matter to memorialize this agreement in a court order, and from time to time you will see this during a divorce, most commonly when there are no children involved.

The second exception is a bit trickier, particularly in today's housing market, and in the aftermath of the subprime lending crisis of several years ago. Remember when I said earlier that any assets or debts acquired during the marriage will most likely he considered marital property? Well, don't forget that <u>debt</u> part. If, by some amazing stroke of luck or your personal connections with a bank or lending institution, you can get a no-money-down mortgage then you have a perfect option available to you. You will not need to use any (presumably marital) funds for a down payment, plus you haven't so much acquired an asset as you've acquired a ton of debt. This can even be used as a strategic move, or a weapon against your spouse, in certain circumstances.

Let's say that you have far more assets than your spouse, such as a pension, IRA, 401(k) or some other large source of funds. At the end of the divorce, when the assets get divided up, you will undoubtedly have to give your spouse a good-sized chunk from these assets (generally at least half). However, the court must also factor in debts along with the assets when dividing up the marital estate. If you were somehow able to acquire a no-money-down mortgage, you would have an immense debt on your side of the spreadsheet which must be taken into account.

Now, I'm not suggesting that the court will give you a dollar for dollar discount when dividing up the estate. Otherwise, everyone under the sun would be buying expensive properties with little or no money down, to offset the amount of money they would have to move to their spouse's side of the spreadsheet. However, it is something the court will consider and will undoubtedly diminish to some extent the number of assets you must transfer to your spouse. The beauty of this strategic move is that you are always free to sell the house after the divorce. Even with no money down, if you've chosen the property carefully, you should be able to sell it after a year or two and come out even after the closing costs. Or, perhaps you genuinely like the property and intend to stay there. Either way you've gained a little more control over the process and put yourself in a much better place from which to make decisions.

However, it's not just real estate that you must be concerned about. Any type of asset acquisition will presumptively raise red flags and could potentially complicate matters. One of the most common assets acquired while a divorce is pending is a new automobile. This can be a positive or negative, depending on the circumstances and the automobile in question. If you are driving a ten or twelve-year-old car and wish to get something more reliable, or something that is not requiring some sort of repair every other month, then it's probably defensible to purchase a new car during a divorce. Your soon-to-be ex-spouse will undoubtedly be outraged, but most of the time the courts won't penalize you for doing so. Just avoid placing a large down payment on the vehicle, as this will usually create instant equity that will then have to be divided. A very, very modest down payment will generally ensure that the vehicle is mostly debt, which will theoretically benefit you at the end of the case, during the division of assets and debts.

There are two caveats to this general rule. Number one, if you and your spouse have historically driven Honda Accords, Toyota Camrys, or some other modest vehicle during the marriage, it would be incredibly foolish to go out and purchase a new BMW, Porsche, or Range Rover. These are the sorts of things that really antagonize a court. Along those lines, if custody and parenting time is a big issue in your divorce, you will completely undercut your own position if you go purchase a Corvette rather than some family-friendly vehicle. Number two, if you have a three or four-year-old vehicle it is never defensible to sell it and purchase a new vehicle during a divorce. This will inevitably be viewed as self-serving, and will attract the scrutiny of the court. If your three or four-year-old vehicle is not particularly family-friendly, then it should be a simple matter to persuade the court or opposing counsel that a more suitable vehicle is needed, especially if you will have a lot of parenting time. In this instance, permission will be far easier to get than forgiveness.

Divorce lawyer history is full of tales of clients who, for some inexplicable reason, decided to purchase boats, airplanes, jet skis, ATVs, timeshares, $20,000 stereo systems, etc. during a divorce. This should go without saying, but let me reiterate that you do not want to be added to the annals of divorce lawyer lore. Always carefully consider your options, be aware of the legal ramifications of any given decision, and consult carefully with your divorce attorney before making any kind of major purchase during your divorce.

MISTAKE #3: NOT LOCKING DOWN YOUR ACCOUNTS

In many regards, this mistake is one of the most crucial. There are so many ways these days for a vengeful spouse to complicate the divorce process or to cause harm purely out of spite. Believe it or not, this is always one of the more difficult things for my divorcing clients to understand. It is sometimes hard to contemplate that their soon-to-be ex-spouse, the person who was their best friend and whom they loved and cherished above all else, is about to turn into their worst enemy. This shouldn't be that difficult to understand. Once those divorce papers get filed, their best interests now lie 180° in the opposite direction of your best interests. Nevertheless, we are all human beings with emotions and feelings, and many times we just don't want to acknowledge this possibility. I think that, in the back of a lot of client's minds, there is a little voice that says, "no matter how bad this divorce gets, I know that my spouse will never go <u>there</u>."

<u>There</u>, of course, is different for different people. But this belief persists that no matter how contested things get and no matter what level of animosity is exhibited. You can at least count on your soon-to-be ex-spouse not to cross some line in the sand. I am here to tell you, <u>do not believe it</u>. The court system is littered with clients who got destroyed during their divorce process because they wouldn't

acknowledge that their spouse was going to go "all out" against them. There is a lot of information and a lot of accounts that you need to take control of immediately when your spouse filed for divorce. For sake of simplicity, I've divided these into three broad categories: financial, lifestyle, and social media. Let's address them one at a time.

The most urgent area in most cases, and arguably the most important, are your financial accounts. If your spouse files for divorce, or if you are planning for filing for divorce you need to lock these accounts down immediately. Here are the crucial things you need to do:

- Take half of the checking and half of the savings accounts, and move them to a separate account or accounts at a <u>new</u> bank or credit union. I can't tell you how many times banks and credit unions have screwed up and allowed a divorcing spouse access to their spouses separate, individual accounts simply because they were all held at the same institution. It is crucial that the new accounts you are going to open be at a separate bank or credit union.
- Make sure that no banking statements, credit card statements, or any other kind of statements get mailed to the residence. Change all your monthly

statements, notifications, and other correspondence to electronic only. Otherwise, you run the risk of your spouse intercepting the mail, and then filling out the change of address form to whichever address she wishes. There's nothing quite like getting a phone call from your credit card company wondering why you haven't paid your balance in four months. Don't give your spouse the opportunity to damage your credit rating any more than is absolutely unavoidable.

- Make sure that your income, particularly if it is directly deposited, goes into your new accounts. Worst case scenario, see if your human resources department or your payroll department can split your paycheck equally between the old and new accounts.

- Make sure you change your ATM pin. Of course, this becomes unnecessary if you have successfully accomplished the previous points in this paragraph. You will simply get a new ATM in a new pin for your new accounts.

- If you have any individual credit cards on which your spouse is an authorized user, contact those credit card companies immediately and have them removed as an authorized user.

- Secure your cellphone with a password and/or numeric passcode.

- If you have any joint credit cards call your credit card company and see if they can split the accounts. If they cannot, ask if they can remove one of the names from the accounts, regardless of whether it's your name or your spouse's name. If they will not do any of the above, let them know that you are currently going through a divorce and ask them to freeze the account so that no new charges may be made. If they won't do that, ask for a supervisor and explain to them that you're going through a divorce and you want your credit limit lowered as low as it can possibly go.

- These include certain non-obvious cards, such as gas station cards, Costco cards, department store cards, etc.

- While not directly financially related, make sure that any official documents that your children may have, such as birth certificates and passports, are moved to a location of your choosing, where your spouse does not have the opportunity to play games with them. This means that you should not play games with them either, but moving them simply gives you more control over possible disagreements, and will prevent your spouse from using them as a weapon against you.

This may seem a little draconian to some of you, but you would be surprised how often a spiteful, angry or hurt spouse chooses, in the heat of the moment, to cut off their own nose to spite their face. At times, I have had my own clients (against my advice) or the opposing party move all the funds from a checking or savings account to a separate account, including sometimes the children's college accounts. Clients have maxed out all their credit cards by writing checks against the credit card accounts, and have used the ATM cards to raid the checking account for hundreds of dollars a day, every day. Litigants have completely canceled credit cards, without notifying their spouse, leading to embarrassing and sometimes humiliating situations for the other spouse. This only throws gasoline on the fire and guarantees a longer, angrier, and more expensive divorce process. I have also seen litigants open credit card accounts in their other spouse's name online, and then go on to run up tens of thousands of dollars in charges. While this is technically a crime, usually the divorce court doesn't want to act on the issue and instead refers you to the district attorney or the states attorney in your area. In my experience, most district attorneys or states attorneys don't want to touch a divorce case with a 10-foot pole, even if actual crimes have been committed. Everything goes much more smoothly when people can act rationally and with a modicum of respect for each other. That being said, if the vast majority of people could do that, I would probably be out of a job. Hence, I urge you to follow the advice listed above. I would also urge everyone who is going through a divorce to obtain a credit report as soon as possible, to determine what their current credit makeup looks like, and to rule out any kind of "phantom" accounts or malicious actions that their spouse might have undertaken.

The next areas that you should address, and which are often overlooked, are what I call "lifestyle accounts." These are things such as country club memberships, gym or fitness memberships, social clubs, etc. This is sometimes a fine line to straddle, because most individuals who are going through a divorce don't necessarily want to broadcast it to everyone they know, and especially not to complete strangers or mere acquaintances. Unfortunately, few things are more embarrassing than showing up at your gym, in your workout clothes, only to be told that your membership is been canceled. Much to your surprise, sometimes they will even tell you it was canceled by you, mere days ago. Along similar lines, showing up for your 7 AM tee time only to find that it's been given away to someone who is still a member of the club can be humiliating, particularly if you've brought the rest of the foursome with you. Some of the most insidious damage is done when an angry spouse tries to sabotage a client's membership and/or standing in a social club. For instance, many major cities have different social clubs, which are a place for individuals of certain solidarities, political persuasions, civic outlooks, or economic strata to meet, dine, socialize, and discuss pertinent issues of the day. On occasion, membership at some of these clubs is integral to one's profession, social standing, or business development. So, it can be particularly devastating when a vengeful spouse interferes, or even sabotages, one's standing and/or membership in one of these clubs or fraternal organizations. Unfortunately, there is no easy way to prevent this without revealing to the administration or management of these entities that you are going through a divorce.

The most discrete way of dealing with these organizations, in my experience, is simply to send them a formal letter letting them know that you're going through divorce, and asking them to kindly contact you on your cell phone if they receive any sort of message or correspondence suggesting a suspension, modification, or cancellation of your membership. This puts the respective organization on notice, and provides a paper trail in case a mistake is subsequently made. Ideally, after you send the letter, you will experience no disruption even if your spouse attempts to torpedo your involvement.

The last area I would like to address, and one that is growing increasingly more critical every year, is social media accounts. The rise and pervasiveness of social media over the past five years has been nothing short of frightening. The amount of information and the unrestricted views into individual's private lives that social media displays on a daily basis is nothing short of stunning. Whether your medium of choice is Facebook, Snapchat, Instagram, or even a more professional arena like LinkedIn, it behooves you to make sure that no one else has access to, or can obtain access to, these accounts.

The first thing you need to do is change the passwords on all your online accounts. Start with your email accounts first. Even if you don't think your spouse has access to them, or knows your passwords, change them anyway. You should have already changed your passwords to your online banking accounts, unless you've already moved your finances to a different financial institution as I suggested earlier in this chapter. To begin, you should make a list of all the social media accounts that you are on currently, and that you used to be on. Now go down the line and change each and every password on all the accounts, without exception. Yes, this means that even if you have a MySpace account back from 2002, and Tom is still your only friend, you need to change the password or completely delete the account. Also, while you are in each respective account please check your settings to make sure that your challenge protocol is also set up to prevent your spouse from accessing it. What is a challenge protocol? A challenge protocol is when you have forgotten your username or password, and the respective social media account sends you a temporary username or a temporary password to get you back on the account. There are usually settings and preferences you can select regarding how you would like to receive this information.

Common examples include emailing you a link to a temporary password or username, sending you a text message with the information, and in some cases, even a telephone call. If you have already changed your email password as outlined previously, then you are probably okay with leaving your challenge protocol selected to email. The most secure option, especially if your mobile phone is locked down, would be to have it sent to you via text message. Once you have this locked down, you can probably sleep a little easier. This will prevent your spouse from hijacking your social media account, fabricating posts or pictures, and attempting to destroy your online life.

That being said, a lot of clients are particularly adept at destroying their online life (and by extension, their offline life) all by themselves. My general suggestion is to disable all your online accounts while the divorce is pending. This means you don't have to delete them or give them up for good, simply make them inactive and unreviewable while the divorce processes ongoing. Many people are unhappy with this advice, which should not be surprising, considering that many people seem incapable of utilizing discretion, politeness, and even common decency in many online interactions. Therefore, I recommend you disable the accounts.

Nothing is worse than a client ripping into their judge, or belittling their soon-to-be ex-spouse online, particularly when opposing counsel shows up at court with screenshots of your social media posts exhibiting these behaviors. Disabling your accounts temporarily also prevents you from doing certain other things which sometimes complicate the divorce process, such as posting pictures of your young children, posting pictures of your new significant other, or having someone else post pictures of activities and situations that you would rather not have displayed for the public (and in particular your future ex-spouse) to see in full detail. Your membership in the "Blackout Brigade" really doesn't need to be displayed online, in full 64-bit color, for all to see. Neither do action shots of you and your spouse's replacement frolicking in some tropical locale, unless you happen to enjoy going to court all the time and giving me more of your hard-earned money. Just don't do it.

MISTAKE #4:
COMPLETELY CUTTING OFF YOUR WIFE FINANCIALLY

This is the perfect time to discuss this mistake, as it is frequently made at the same time people take action in some of the areas listed in the prior chapter. In fact, this is probably the single most common mistake that men make in a divorce, particularly if they are the breadwinner. Sadly, it's a completely understandable mistake. If you are not the one who filed for divorce, your most common reaction is to be hurt, to be confused, to be angry, and to lash out in any way that you can. Please try and resist this temptation. If you do something along these lines, please <u>undo</u> them once you've calmed down.

If you are the one who has filed for divorce, perhaps this was part of your grand plan to immediately take the upper hand and to put your spouse in a horrible bargaining position. This behavior usually stems from a misunderstanding of how the court system works and what the court is likely to do in these situations. Most states and court systems today have statutes or provisions that prevent this sort of maneuver from lasting very long. Gone are the days when the breadwinner could completely cut off the other spouse and effectively strong-arm them into some sort of settlement. If that was your grand plan, please understand that this is a <u>horrible</u> plan, one that will not work and will most likely antagonize the court right from the start. The last thing you want is the judge in your case to think you're a douchebag right from the get-go.

Unfortunately, a certain percentage of clients suffer from a particularly debilitating condition. People who suffer from this condition exhibit a range of symptoms including, but not limited to: poor impulse control, failure to think things through, self-destructive behaviors, and an inadvertent desire to pay me a lot of money. This condition is known as FTBS, or, Fuck This Bitch Syndrome. This syndrome begins to manifest itself when someone's wife files for divorce. At this point a range of emotions begin to flood the husband's mind, starting from, "I can't believe this is happening to me" to, "I can't believe she is doing this to me" and then eventually, "How dare she do this to me!" The emotions continue to cascade from this point and inevitably spiral downward until the husband in question is willing to do anything in his power to hurt his soon-to-be ex-wife, regardless of the consequences to her or to him.

No retaliation is too severe, no consequence too damaging, and no action too odious that will prevent a client suffering from FTBS from making a poor decision. Unfortunately, there is no cure for FTBS. However, there are definitely ways to treat this condition. If you feel that you might be suffering from FTBS, I would urge you to immediately schedule a meeting with your attorney. If you don't have an attorney, I would recommend strongly that you get one immediately, before you become the iceberg that sinks your own Titanic. All humor aside, there are many valid reasons why you do not want to totally cut off your spouse financially during a divorce.

The first reason is one that we have already discussed. Judges are people too, and they experience the full range of human emotions just like you and I do. The last thing you want to do at the very beginning of a divorce case is to irritate or antagonize the judge. On top of the court having an unfavorable impression of you from the start, you also make your attorney's job much tougher, as they will have to fight an uphill battle to redeem your reputation and persuade the judge that you are not, in fact, a douchebag.

The second reason flows logically from the first. If you antagonize the court at the outset of your case, and if you've taken a drastic step which will inevitably produce a reaction in your wife and her attorney, you will make this divorce case a lot more expensive. To put it bluntly, you will pay for doing this. You will pay me to go to court and respond to the inevitable motion your wife's attorney will file. You will probably pay your wife's attorney, because your wife is entitled to use marital funds for her fees and you have just sequestered all the funds. You may even wind up paying your wife some extra money, as the court may begin to sympathize with your wife's plight if you begin the case acting in this manner.

What you do by cutting off your spouse financially at the beginning of a divorce case is to presumptively escalate not just financial matters, but every matter that will come up for the length of the case. By showing the court and your soon-to-be ex-spouse that you are not going to act in an adult manner and are going to fight at every chance you get, you send the message to her attorney and to the court that this divorce is going to be a "knock-down, drag-out" slugfest and that they should proceed accordingly. Allow me to let you in on a little secret: clients in a divorce case will not trust each other (I mean, it's a divorce). But very often the attorneys in the case have known each other for years, have had numerous cases with each other, and can work together efficiently to reach a resolution that benefits everyone. However, by starting a case with the aforementioned maneuver you send a message to the other attorney that you have no problem disregarding your own attorney's advice, or that you have no hesitation acting before consulting with your attorney. Either message guarantees that the other attorney is going to have to change their approach, dig in, and prepare for World War III. And wars are <u>expensive</u>.

If you have children, there is another reason you don't want to do this. Whether we like to admit it or not, children (even young children) are very perceptive and usually know more about what's going on in their parents' lives than we realize. If you start the divorce off by completely cutting off your spouse financially, think about the message that you're sending the children. Is this the example you want to set for your children regarding how to interact with their mother? Is this really the behavior that you want to model for them? If it's okay for you to treat their mother like this, why isn't it okay for them to do so? Believe me, these are behaviors that you do not want to exhibit for your kids. Even if deep down inside you absolutely hate her guts, you don't want the children to think that kind of behavior is acceptable. The best way to stop them from seeing that behavior is to not behave that way, especially since there are so many easier ways to protect and stabilize your financial situation during a divorce. If you really want to set an example for your children, follow the rules about dividing up the checking and savings accounts as set forth in the prior chapter, and then throw your soon-to-be ex-wife a little something extra every month, just to show there's no ill will.

If you are thinking about cutting your wife off financially, and you have also left or are planning to leave the marital residence, please be aware that your children will undoubtedly perceive this as complete abandonment. If you decide to move out of the marital house, you may well be able to sit down with the children and have a discussion with them about how you and their mom are having problems, and how you need to take a break from each other, and how you still love them and will be spending as much time with him as you can, etc. But if this happens in conjunction with you taking all the funds, your words will ring hollow.

It's hard for them to take your platitudes and heartfelt statements seriously when their mom is complaining she doesn't have enough money to buy them breakfast cereal, or pay for their soccer team, or afford a hot lunch at school that day. If you are planning on leaving the house, or if you've already left, cutting your wife off

Joseph F. Emmerth

financially means cutting the children off financially, by default. Don't do it.

Don't assume that by telling your wife upfront that you're going to cut her off, or by giving her a "heads up", that you will be absolved of your actions or that everything will be peachy. While it is a good rule not to keep your spouse in the dark financially (even during a divorce), telling her in advance of something that will universally be construed as poor behavior buys you no good will from her or the court. This is such an easy mistake to avoid, and yet men keep making it over and over again. This just goes to demonstrate the power of emotion in the divorce process. If treated like a business decision, it would become obvious that the best course of action is not to completely cut off your wife financially.

For instance, if you took $40,000 out of the accounts and left your wife with nothing, certain things will likely happen. She will have her attorney file a motion. You will pay your attorney $5,000.00 to defend your actions in court. You will most likely pay your wife's attorney $5,000.00 in attorney's fees, and then you will most likely equally divide the remaining funds with your wife. So, instead of each of you having $20,000 in your account to start off the case, with the court having an unbiased opinion of each of you, now you will each only have $15,000 in your account, and the judge will approach this case thinking you're an asshole from the start. Unfortunately, there is no medication for FTBS. Your best chance of avoiding it is to get with your attorney in the hope that you can prevent it from occurring in the first place.

MISTAKE #5:
SHUTTING DOWN OR IGNORING
THE PROCESS

Perhaps your problem isn't anger or impulse control. Perhaps your feelings about the divorce do not fall under the "retribution/get even" portion of the spectrum. Maybe this divorce caught you completely off-guard. Maybe you didn't see it coming at all. Maybe it is as surprising as a meteorite falling from the sky and landing in your backyard. If this is the case, you have my sympathies. It's one thing when the marriage has been headed south for quite a while and everyone has known there are problems for a long time. It's another thing entirely when you are completely blindsided by a divorce.

When this is the case, there is a certain percentage of clients who simply can't deal with the situation. In other words, they shut down, mentally and emotionally. They ignore the process and refuse to admit that any sort of legal proceeding is happening. This is a classic example of denial. Because the knowledge that their marriage has failed and is ending is so painful, they simply refuse to acknowledge it at all. Initially their mind is overwhelmed with feelings of shock and pain: "My life is over", "How could she do this to me?", "She's going to take my kids!" These types of thoughts are very common, and it's not out of the question that depression sets in, along with the denial. For some clients, complete and utter numbness is preferable than acknowledging and addressing the emotions that they are feeling. Clients who react to a divorce in this manner frequently exhibit a bizarre range of reactions (or non-reactions) and behaviors.

One way in which clients frequently react is to think that their spouse is not serious. In this scenario, the husband firmly believes that his wife has made a mistake and that she will eventually "come around" and change her mind. This husband will go about business as usual, dropping the kids off at school, lounging around the house, discussing day-to-day issues with his wife, and pretty much ignoring the legal process. Sometimes the husband may even "up his game" and act like a better or improved version of himself in a vain attempt to show her that things really aren't that bad and that she has made a mistake by filing for divorce. The problem with this approach (other than the fact that it ignores the reality on the ground) is that the legal system does not care whether you are acknowledging the divorce. There is a common and far-ranging misconception about the divorce process, which is best summed up as, "She can't divorce me if I don't agree to it/sign the papers." I've often wondered where this misperception comes from. I seem to recall, while watching old black and white western movies in my youth, that occasionally a character would yell out (presumably at their spouse), "I won't give you a divorce!" or, "why won't you give me a divorce!" Maybe back in the days of the Wild West you actually needed your spouse's consent to get a divorce. However, much like the cowboys and Indians of our youth, those days are long gone.

States and court systems now have laws and rules that specifically deal with situations in which a spouse can't be found, or a spouse refuses to participate at all. In Illinois, the state in which I practice, once you file for divorce you must serve your spouse with the divorce papers. Once they are served, your spouse has thirty days to either get their own attorney or to file a form with the court, which lets the court know they will be representing themselves in the divorce. If they do neither of these things, the spouse who filed for divorce is entitled to file what we call a motion for default. This motion asks the court to find that the other spouse is in default, and to allow the divorce to proceed without their participation. Provided the spouse can show proof of service of the divorce papers, this motion is almost always granted, and the divorce will proceed without the other spouse's participation. In that rare instance where the

other spouse literally cannot be found, the courts will eventually allow the other spouse to serve the missing spouse via publication, which means taking out a small ad in a local newspaper for a set length of time, informing the other spouse that they have filed for divorce. If the missing spouse does not respond within a preset timeframe, the court will hold them in default of the divorce will proceed without them.

I know it seems bizarre than a spouse would simply choose to completely ignore the process, or act as if it's not really happening, but I can tell you from experience that there have been cases where the spouse has been defaulted and the divorce has been granted, yet the husband continues to live in the marital home and act as if the parties are still married. These people eventually must be removed by law enforcement, and it is not pretty. Assumptions like, "if they can't serve me it can't happen, right?" and, "if I don't participate then it can't happen" are relics of the past, and you place yourself at a real disadvantage if you cling to these outdated misconceptions.

A second variation on this theme is when a husband tells himself that, "he will be able to talk her out of this." Many husbands will tell themselves that their wife is prone to flights of fancy, rarely thinks things through, and needs to be shown that the option she has chosen is not a good one. Husbands in this case will essentially attempt a strategy of wearing their wife down via constant discussions about how they've made a mistake, how they don't really want this, how things will be much worse if they get divorced, etc.

Husbands in this scenario will also refuse to participate in the process, either out of an attempt to demonstrate to their wife that the divorce is a mistake, or that they are supremely confident that she will "come to her senses." Believe it or not, once in a very great while, the wife will give in and withdraw her divorce petition. However, this only guarantees that she will file for divorce again within the next year or two, and this time will not be dissuaded from following through with the process.

A third variation on this scenario is a bit more underhanded. In this scenario, the wife is well aware that the husband has shut down, and is ignoring the process. So, the wife encourages the husband not to participate, telling him that even though they are going through a divorce they can keep working on the marriage and attempt to salvage the relationship. The wife will hold out incentives for the husband to sign the papers, such as, "we can continue going to counseling" or, "we can keep working on this relationship and get remarried later." Sadly, many men fall for this gambit, their wives' hollow promises providing just enough hope to overcome their feelings of denial and avoidance. Perhaps she's telling you, "I know the divorce papers say X, Y, and Z, but that doesn't mean that we have to follow them after the divorce." Or, perhaps she's telling you that, even though her proposed parenting schedule only lets you see the kids every other weekend, once the divorce is finalized, "you can see them any time you want to." Do not fall for these lies. Your spouse is taking advantage of your pain and emotional state to manipulate you into a settlement that is in her best interests, not yours.

I would be remiss at this point if I didn't mention mental health professionals. It is common to feel emotions of sadness and some level of depression during a divorce. That doesn't make you weak; it merely makes you human. If you are feeling down, or feeling like you want to crawl into a hole and die, then go see a therapist immediately. Many men (much more than women) refuse to see a mental health professional because of social conditioning and perceived stigmas against doing so. Your mental health is too important to ignore during this process. Please go see a therapist today.

Do not expect your divorce attorney to be your therapist. While it is true that divorce attorneys, more than most other types of attorneys, must be counselors to their clients in addition to litigators, it is unreasonable and unwise to expect your lawyer to provide the mental health assistance that you require. Not only will seeing a therapist be cheaper, on average, then talking to your divorce attorney about your feelings, but you really deserve a professional dedicated to your mental health to help you through this rough time in your life. I get it, I do. Nobody wants to go see a therapist. But by the same token, nobody wants to be sitting in a divorce attorney's office, either. Sometimes life dictates that you seek out a professional. Don't be afraid of doing so simply because you think the area of that professional's expertise reflects poorly on you. This is about you, and being the best, most healthy you that you can be. There is nothing to be ashamed of in that.

In summary, ignoring things and/or pretending that things are not happening is no way to live your life. Just because ostriches don't appear to have marital problems, that doesn't mean sticking your head in the sand is a good strategy. Being fully present in your life (and by extension, your divorce) is the best approach. As Woody Allen once said, "Eighty percent of success is showing up." Don't be a casual observer of your own life. Don't stand on the sidelines while you watch things happen to you. Make things happen. Be an active participant in your own life. Choose your own course and direction. Be the captain of your own ship.

MISTAKE #6:
USING THE SAME ATTORNEY OR NOT HIRING AN ATTORNEY AT ALL

This mistake is perfectly understandable in some situations. That being said, it is still a mistake. There are many reasons you may want to use the same attorney as your soon-to-be ex-spouse. In fact, your ex-spouse might be urging you to do so in certain circumstances. The most common reason for choosing to use the same attorney is an obvious one: cost. If both you and your wife are very frugal, or from very modest means, the thought of having to pay two separate attorneys can be very daunting. Even if you and your wife are not frugal, sometimes the idea of using the same attorney can be appealing, based on a flawed belief about divorce attorneys in general. There is an idea that exists among a certain percentage of the population, namely that divorce attorneys are only interested in one thing: fighting over everything in court and extracting as much money from you as possible.

I will grant you that there are disreputable individuals in any profession, from used car salesman to neurosurgeons. The law is no different. However, I think the public at large would be shocked to discover how much of our typical days are spent trying to talk client <u>out</u> of doing things. Rather than treating the client like an ATM, most of our days are spent talking with clients about the best strategy to employ, listening to their ideas and offering more efficient and cheaper solutions, or dealing with the ramifications of their poor choices in the courtroom. Most divorce attorneys that I know are more than happy to talk themselves out of work if it is in the client's best interest. Most our referrals come from previous clients who were happy with our services. Hence, it's not in our best interests to artificially stir up trouble and prolong cases for no reason. Our job is to try and accomplish the client's goals as efficiently as we can, and with as little hostility as possible. The problem that results from using the same attorney solely to save costs is the same problem that results from doing anything based on costs alone. If you purchase the cheapest car, take the lowest construction bid, get the cheapest haircut, eat at the cheapest restaurant, or purchase the cheapest set of tools, you are undoubtedly going to receive an inferior product and/or have an awful experience in the long-term.

Another reason people sometimes choose to use the same attorney is that they feel they don't have anything to fight over, or they have no assets and debts that need divided. This is particularly true in short marriages with no children. Occasionally, these people are correct. Sometimes there is nothing to fight over, and there are no issues that need to be litigated. However, in this case there is an entire class of professionals that are there to help you out. These people are called mediators. Every county, court system, and Bar Association should have a list of mediators, or can refer you to one upon request. These people are true neutrals, meaning they do not represent either one of you in the process, and are there merely to facilitate putting your desires into a format that the court will accept to get you divorced. Often these professionals will work on a flat fee basis, or be much, much less expensive than hiring a divorce attorney to run your case. If this is the route that seems most appropriate to you I would caution you to consider a few items.

First off, please do not think that downloading forms from a website such as LegalZoom, or purchasing some high-tech mediation equivalent like WeVorce, is a valid substitute for a trained mediator. Many people who try these services wind up eventually going to a mediator or an attorney anyway, once they realize these products are not sufficient for their needs. Secondly, you must bear in mind that a mediator is not working in your best interests, or your spouse's best interests, they are merely a neutral third-party who will assist you in trying to put your agreement on paper. A mediator may not always be aware of the rules, "quirks", or best practices of the court system in which you reside. Therefore, to achieve the best results from a mediation, please make sure that your mediator is also a licensed attorney.

A lot of people assume that, if they've been referred to a mediator from a Bar Association or a court system, that said mediator will be an attorney. This is not always true. In a lot of jurisdictions, mediators are not required to be attorneys, and can instead be mental health professionals, accountants, or members of other professions. While these professionals all have their respective strengths and skills, only a mediator who is an attorney will be aware of the particular pitfalls you might run into with your agreement, or the particular wording and preferences of the judges you will appear before. So, for best results, make sure your mediator is also an attorney.

However, most of the time divorcing couples are not correct, and they actually do have assets, debts, and other issues that do need to be addressed. Let's be clear about what "using the same attorney" really means. What it means in 99.9% of cases is that your spouse has gone out and found an attorney, who will be representing her best interests and her interests alone. They will be friendly to you in the office when you meet and they will discuss things in a friendly and moderate tone as they go through your wife's proposal. But they do not care one iota about what's best for you or what's in your best interests. They will phrase things in such a way that the settlement appears beneficial for both of you, and upon reviewing the papers you may even agree that everything looks good.

But you are not a lawyer, do not know what the law says in this area, and don't know what a court would likely do in regard to the assets and debts in your particular situation. The attorney's responsibility is to your wife, not to you, and the attorney might casually mention several times that they hope you understand that they do not represent you in this matter. Don't let the friendly atmosphere and the amicable tone deceive you. You may very well be getting hosed. The sad thing is, you might never know it, because you don't have anyone on your side giving you independent legal advice. Therefore, it is crucial that you get your own attorney, or at a minimum take the documents and pay an attorney for an hour or two of their time to get their unbiased and objective opinion.

Sometimes people don't want to hire their own attorney because they feel like they are more than up to the task themselves. Decades of watching Perry Mason, Law and Order, Boston Legal, or Suits makes them feel like they have more than enough knowledge and legal acumen to represent themselves in this process. I have to believe that these individuals are the same people who, as children, tried jumping off the roof in a makeshift cape because they thought they were Superman. Those that survived the experience without injury have unfortunately learned the wrong lesson.

There is a saying among divorce lawyers that goes like this: "Anyone who represents themselves has a fool for a client." It might surprise people to find out that most divorce attorneys won't even represent themselves in their own divorce, even though they do have the knowledge and legal acumen to do so. This is for a simple reason. There are so many emotions, feelings, and issues intrinsic to a divorce that blending the personal and the professional is simply too much to handle. Simply put, it is nearly impossible to look at things in an objective manner when they are happening to you and when they involve a gamut of powerful emotions. If a trained and experienced divorce attorney won't represent themselves, then a layperson certainly shouldn't do so. I have heard potential clients say things such as, "I'm excellent at arguing," or, "surely the judge will listen to common sense," or, "the law seems pretty straightforward." Statements like these always make me smile. Anytime I step up in court and see that my opposing party is representing themselves, I mentally start licking my chops. This is because I am about to work them over like a side of beef, "Rocky" style. It has been said many times that experience is the best teacher, but it's a fool's school; and this is never more true than in a courtroom.

It may surprise self-represented litigants that most of what goes on in a divorce case is not arguing. Even if you do happen to be good at arguing, rarely do you know what to argue about, when to argue it, or how to argue it, and in a way that is not going to annoy the judge. I, on the other hand, appear in front of this particular judge on a regular basis, have gotten to know his or her tendencies and preferences over the years, and have years and years of experience in what to argue, when to argue it, and how to argue it. If you choose to represent yourself, the deck is stacked against you from the beginning. It may also surprise people to find out that not much about the law is based on common sense. Decades and decades ago, before state legislatures addressed areas of the law with legislation and statutes, most of our court proceedings were based on what is called the Common Law. In my opinion, not much of that was based on common sense, either. In any event, today we have laws and statutes that specifically address various areas of the law.

In Illinois, where I practice, we have the Illinois Marriage and Dissolution of Marriage Act. It is full of rules, regulations, factors, formulas, and many other specialized directives and protocols for dealing with a divorce case. This statute was created, underwent numerous revisions, and has been debated extensively by attorneys. I can assure you that a layperson's idea of "common sense" played very little part in the process. In addition to this, the law frequently undergoes changes. In fact, our statute has had three or four significant revisions in the past five years alone. Bar associations and court systems have organized numerous multi-day seminars to explain these complex changes to divorce practitioners. Good luck keeping up with them, and understanding their impact, if you are a layperson. In short, anyone who feels that the law is straightforward has not spent very much time reviewing the law.

Perhaps I have persuaded you not to represent yourself at this point. Good, that's a start. But let's say you still don't want to incur the expense of hiring your own separate attorney, and decide to simply use your spouse's attorney, albeit with close attention to detail and a high level of scrutiny. Let me reiterate it one more time: you are not a professional. You have deliberately put yourself in a position where the person sitting across from you, the person representing your wife, is a professional. This is a recipe for disaster. Let me try and put this in perspective. Would you perform surgery on yourself? Of course not, you're not a doctor (and even if you were, you probably wouldn't). Would you rebuild the engine on your Porsche? Of course not, you're not a Porsche mechanic. Would you run the wiring and install the electrical system in your own home? Of course not, you're not an electrician. Yet you're going to sit at the table, with an experienced divorce attorney who represents your wife, and try and represent yourself? Tell me again how this seems like a good idea?

I hope you can see that you are way out of your element in this situation. You are essentially playing a sport where your opponent is the referee. Did you know that, even on the day you stand in front of the judge and get divorced, if the judge sees that you are representing yourself they will offer to stop the proceedings to allow you time to consult with and/or get your own attorney? That's how important this is. Protect yourself, hire your own attorney.

MISTAKE #7:
IMMEDIATELY "MOVING ON" TO
THE NEXT RELATIONSHIP

Next to cutting off your spouse financially, none of the mistakes men make in divorce have the potential to ensure a messy, hostile, take-no-prisoners divorce more than this one. It's one thing if infidelity has led to the divorce. When your wife discovers you've been cheating, more often than not, you can brace yourself for a healthy dose of "woman scorned" behavior. And let's face it, you knew it was coming, no surprises there, whole books have been written on that subject. No, what I'm going to discuss in this chapter is when you decide to immediately replace your wife with another relationship.

When you suddenly appear with a new girlfriend, boyfriend, or significant other mere weeks after filing for divorce, it sends several messages to your soon to be ex-spouse. The first message it sends is that you have replaced her. Despite your five, ten, twenty years together, she is merely a cog in a machine that can be swapped out at any time, with no problem or complication. This produces a countervailing response in your wife, namely, she will make it her mission in life to show you that you will not be replacing her that easily, and that your callousness towards her position in this relationship is about to be punished. In other words, if you think that she just going to sit there and accepted being perfunctorily labeled a "recyclable", then you've got another thing coming. Reasonable proposals she normally would have agreed to, common sense suggestions that she would normally go along with, and any chance of amicable behavior will now go out the window.

But why, you may ask? "This marriage has been dead for a long time and I moved on mentally a long time ago." Both of those things may be true, but you miss the point. Because the other message it sends to your soon to be ex-wife is that you don't even respect her. While the marriage, in fact, may have been dead for years, marriages mean different things to different people. Perhaps divorce is unheard of on your wife's side of the family. Perhaps "doing this to her" means that not only will you be leaving her, but that her entire extended family will now view her as a pariah and failure. Or perhaps being married to you has conferred a social status on your wife that she otherwise could not have hoped to achieve on her own. Maybe you divorcing her now means she won't be welcome at the yacht club, or country club, or at various other organizations or social settings. For her, you have essentially banished her to a lower social stratum, complete with loss of public or social status and probably many of her "friends" and acquaintances. Maybe you divorcing her means that she must move to a different town or city, quit going to her favorite restaurants, or change the lifestyle she has had for years.

For many people, losing a spouse is only one small part of a divorce. If you compound it by parading around her "replacement" so soon after "firing the opening shot" in this divorce case, you are probably rubbing more salt into the wound than she can reasonably be expected to calmly accept. Remember, intellectually knowing that the marriage is over is vastly different than being able to cope with it in day-to-day reality. This means a drastically more expensive divorce if you choose to do this.

Another complication that potentially arises when you immediately leap into a new relationship is the interplay with your children. If you start bringing the children around your new significant other, you can be sure that they will see this new person as their mother's replacement. If they don't, you can bet she will be sure to tell them. Courts are also unpredictable in these situations. Some judges will frown on bringing the children around this new person if you've only been dating for a few months, and will be very upset if you allow this person to spend the night while the children are present. Other courts don't seem to care very much. Hence, the potential exists to somewhat alienate your children and possibly antagonize the judge. Best practice is to simply not do it at all.

In addition to the above, let me mention again the legal concept that exists in some jurisdictions called "Dissipation." Dissipation occurs when one spouse uses funds for non-marital purposes during the divorce. A good example of this is buying your new significant other jewelry, or taking them on a vacation. I can recall incidents where someone bought their new beau a sports car, or set them up in a penthouse apartment—while the divorce was still in progress. This was a very bad idea. Unless you have more money than God, this will come back to bite you. If a court finds that you have dissipated funds, you are generally responsible for reimbursing your spouse for a percentage of the funds spent (usually at least 50%). Depending on how much you have spent on your new relationship, after you've reimbursed your soon to be ex-spouse their portion, you may very well find yourself with enough funds to buy a newspaper and a McDouble. Best practice would be to pay cash (no paper trail) or to simply have them pay their own way for now. Super-best practice would be to not have to deal with this possibility at all.

There are other possible disadvantages to immediately moving on to a new relationship (I know, they just keep on coming, don't they?). This one involves the actual individual you are now seeing. Sometimes your new significant other, well aware that they are now in the proverbial driver's seat, decides to insert themselves into the process. This is another recipe for disaster. Please understand, they have absolutely no "skin in the game", and therefore they feel free to give you all kinds of bad advice regarding your divorce. "My friend's attorney got this for her/him," or, "You should tell your attorney to do...." or, "If I was you, I would play hardball," are all frequent admonitions from your new squeeze.

If you have decided to immediately jump into a new relationship, then I can't stop you. But please understand that your new addition is going to be giving you advice on what's best <u>for them</u>, not you. Often, they will see themselves in direct competition with your soon-to-be ex for limited resources (you and your money). Even if they happen to be a very selfless, caring individual who sincerely desires what's best for you (and not just for them), they are still going to be viewing things through the prism of their life experience, and thus might not be all that helpful to you during this trying time. Essentially, the last thing you need in your ear is another voice that doesn't know what they are talking about.

Additionally, it should be said that going through a divorce is usually the worst thing that a person will go through, absent losing a child. So why would you add to the stress of an already difficult time by taking on the challenge and obligations of a new relationship? Not the best decision, to be sure. Believe me, you will have more than enough on your plate to deal with during the divorce. The last thing you need to add to the equation is more stress.

Please allow yourself some time to recalibrate to being single. You are going through an incredibly tough time. You owe it to yourself to allow some time to process and adjust to your new life. Maybe you'll enjoy being single for a while. Maybe you would really benefit from using this time to reflect and focus on personal growth, or on expanding your horizons, or doing things you were never able to do while married. This could be your opportunity to travel the world, or volunteer, or catch up on some long overdue reading, or even simple R&R. There's no need to immediately jump back in to the pressure and obligations that come with a new relationship. Be good to yourself.

Don't make the transition harder. Don't allow your focus to be distracted during this critical time.

This is a good time to address the other side of the coin, and impart some advice to those of you who did decide to move on prior to filing for divorce. Don't think of this new person as a lifeline, or as an upgrade over your current spouse. Statistics consistently tell us that this relationship is even more likely to fail than your first marriage. More likely than not, there will come a day when you find yourself on the other side of things, and discover that your new beau has, in fact, moved on and replaced you. All I ask is that you don't act surprised. After all, they cheated by dating you while you were still married. What on earth made you think they wouldn't do it again? The best predictor of future behavior is past behavior. If they cheated to be with you, odds are one day they will cheat again. Just know what you're getting into before you decide to go down that road.

MISTAKE #8:
DISPARAGING YOUR WIFE IN FRONT OF THE CHILDREN, OR USING THE CHILDREN AS MESSENGERS

There is nothing quite like a divorce to bring out the worst in people. People will often do things during a divorce that they would never, in a million years, even consider doing under normal circumstances. Traditional roles break down, responsible patterns of behavior vanish, and people frequently behave in incredibly childish ways, either out of frustration or desperation. One area that frequently exhibits displays of poor behavior is your relationship with your children. Common sense would dictate that you leave the children out of the nuts and bolts and day-to-day struggles of the divorce, even if that divorce involves a custody battle.

Children are not emotionally equipped or mature enough to understand and deal with all the emotions that accompany a divorce, nor should they be asked to deal with it even if they are mature enough to understand and deal with those emotions. The divorce is a failed relationship between you and your spouse, not you and your kids. Nonetheless, there remains a large proportion of divorcing parents that try and interject the children into the equation at every opportunity. This poor behavior generally falls into one of two categories: a) using the children as messengers; or b) using the children as sounding boards and or confidants.

Let's address the first issue: using the children as messengers. The first thing I would admonish you to do is to be an adult. You are not in junior high school. The days of scribbling notes on pieces of paper and passing them down the line to someone else is over. If you have an issue with someone, or you need to discuss serious matters with someone, then you need to discuss it with them <u>directly</u>. Ideally, you should be able to talk to your soon-to-be ex-spouse face-to-face, even if it is uncomfortable to do so. However, I understand that sometimes this simply isn't going to happen, either due to the amount of anger or bitterness inherent in the failing relationship. If this is the case with your divorce you have other options. The first option is the telephone. All you have to do is pick up the phone and call your soon-to-be ex-spouse. You can then have a conversation about whatever issue you need to, without the added stress of having to look at them or be near them. If things to get heated, or uncomfortable, or threaten to spiral out of control, all you have to do is hang up.

The second option is email. You can sit down in front of your computer, calmly type a detailed message, and even save that message to come back and review again before you send it to your spouse. This affords you the opportunity to revise and sharpen your message, so that your thoughts and ideas are expressed clearly and concisely, and without any sarcasm or anger that might bubble to the surface during a face-to-face meeting or telephone call. You may have noticed that at no point in time in this section have I suggested that an option is to use the children as messengers. That's because it is never a good option. There are so many ways to communicate with your spouse these days that there is never a need to put the children in the middle of this process by using them as messengers. Children should not be privy to adult conversations, especially ones that involve them, or that may affect them indirectly. You need to leave them out of it, period. Needing an intermediary to communicate simple messages to your spouse is a sign of immaturity and weakness. Be an adult, and leave adult functions to the adults.

The second issue involves using your children as confidants, or sounding boards for the divorce process. This frequently manifests itself by one spouse bad-mouthing the other spouse in front of the children, or in some cases, directly to the children. This is an awful, horrible thing to do. I get it, you and your spouse are not getting along. Not only do you not like each other, you might even actively hate each other at this moment. But I can guarantee you your children don't share your feelings toward your spouse. You may feel like your wife is an evil person, or your nemesis, or the one who is caused all this havoc in your life. But to your children, she is still "Mom." Just because you can't stand her, doesn't mean they feel the same way. They may love her more now than ever, especially if this divorce is rocking their whole world to the core.

Disparaging their mom, or attempting to portray her as a bad person is only going to create more stress and more issues in their lives than they already have. They may even come to resent you for doing it, and you may inadvertently force them to "choose sides" if you harp on their mother constantly. If you are constantly bashing her in front of them, and she is not responding in kind, she will immediately become the sympathetic figure in their eyes. They will rally around her and start viewing you as the bad guy in this scenario. Sadly, you will deserve it, at least in part.

Conversely, if you are complementary towards their mother in your conversations with them, or even if you simply refuse to say anything bad about her (even if they try and bait you into doing so) you will be a much better person in their eyes. It doesn't matter if you hate her guts, just don't convey that feeling to the children or express it in front of them. If their mother is bad mouthing you, then you become the sympathetic figure. If she isn't, then congratulations, both of you are keeping the children out of the middle, which is what you should be doing anyway.

Keeping the children out of the middle of the conflict is not only best for the children, but it should benefit you in court as well, particularly if there is a custody fight ongoing. Courts hate to see one spouse or the other involving the children in the divorce or actively bashing the other parent in front of the children. In some jurisdictions, courts appoint an attorney for the children, or an attorney to do an investigation and report back to the court with recommendations about parenting time and decision-making authority. These individuals will speak with your children, so if one or both of you are disparaging the other, it will certainly come out. It will almost certainly color and influence that individual's view towards you and towards the custodial recommendation. This is one of those areas where being on your best behavior is not only its own reward, but should put you in the best position to get the best result possible in court.

One final word on this subject: the topics and advice given in this chapter don't just apply to minor children. Perhaps you've been married for thirty or forty years, and now unfortunately find yourself in the middle of a divorce. Maybe your children are in their 20s or even 30s, with children of their own. It is still wildly inappropriate to use them as confidants in this scenario. You should not be bouncing ideas off your adult children, or confiding in them the sordid details or emotionally-laden feelings regarding the end of the marriage. To them, you are still mom and dad, no matter how old you are or how long they've been out of the nest. It is unfair to put them in that position, and you will only make them uncomfortable or perhaps even resentful if you do so. At this stage in your life you should have plenty of friends or colleagues to talk to about these issues. Utilize them. If for some reason you don't, then go see a therapist. If that makes you uncomfortable, then try a pastor, priest, or other religious figure in your faith. These people often have special training, and a mandate to assist people going through tough times like these. Seek them out and use them.

MISTAKE #9:
HIDING SECRETS FROM YOUR ATTORNEY

Many of the mistakes in this book revolve around several common themes, such as not unnecessarily antagonizing your spouse, not making yourself look bad in the court's eyes, or not doing things that will drastically increase the cost of your divorce. However, there are a few mistakes that don't fit neatly into any of these categories, primarily because they are so mind-boggling that it's hard to explain why anyone would make them in the first place. One of those mistakes is the subject of this chapter.

For some reason, and God only knows why, there is a small but consistent percentage of clients who feel that they need to withhold information from their attorney. This is commonly referred to as secret keeping. At first glance, you might think that this mistake is easy to explain. Clients are going through very chaotic and stressful times, and the issues involved are very personal and emotional. Who wouldn't want to keep those things private? This line of reasoning breaks down under closer scrutiny, however. Let me propose some other scenarios to you, and you decide if the people in them are behaving rationally or irrationally:

Scenario one: your car or truck has been making strange sounds for about a month. It has gotten to the point where not only is it making noises, but it's shuddering and

78

sometimes refusing to start. You decide to take it to the mechanic, and once you arrive he asks you to describe what's been happening. However, this is your automobile, and you feel uncomfortable telling him exactly what it has been doing. After all, this is your personal vehicle, and you have a right to privacy. So, you just tell the mechanic, "it's just not acting right." You don't tell him about the noises it has been making, or the shuddering and starting issues it has been having recently.

Scenario two: you've been feeling really run down for the past few weeks. You've been having problems sleeping, you have lost your appetite, and now you're starting to get headaches with disturbing frequency. You make an appointment to go see your doctor. When you go to your appointment, you don't disclose any of your symptoms, and simply tell your treating physician that, "you just haven't felt like yourself lately." You refuse to discuss any details with the doctor.

Do the people in the scenarios listed above sound like rational people? Or do they sound like complete and utter morons who are only making their professional's job harder and costlier for them in the long run? The answer is clearly the latter. In fact, while you were reading through the scenarios I'm fairly confident that most of you were thinking, "what the hell are these people thinking?" Or, "what are these people doing?" A lot of people would go so far as to say that the people in these scenarios are insane, because they are clearly acting against their own best interests. Yet, there remains the small but consistent percentage of clients that do exactly that with their own attorneys.

From an attorney's perspective, this is one of the dumbest things you could ever do. Yet a certain percentage of clients continue to do it, without fail. There is a scene in the movie Fight Club where Tyler Durden addresses his new recruits with a megaphone, telling them, "You are not special. You are not a beautiful and unique snowflake." A lot of divorce attorneys feel the same way about their clients from time to time. While it is true that every case has its own quirks, flow, and dynamics, believe me when I tell you that you are not going to surprise your attorney with some revelation that you might be hiding away. Any divorce attorney who's been practicing more than a decade has quite literally seen it all; every kind of infidelity, poor decision, illegal behavior, criminal activity, kinky quirk, etc. If you felt bad enough to go see your doctor, you wouldn't lie to them, and if your vehicle was operating so poorly that you felt the need to take it to the mechanic, you wouldn't lie to them either. So why would you lie to your attorney?

I am only here to help you. My mission, both philosophically and legally, is to serve your best interests. A lot of people don't realize that the practice of law is really a service industry. The client has a need, and they hire me (usually by the hour) to work on their behalf to solve the problem. A high degree of skill and good customer service are what I strive to provide. It becomes incredibly hard to do that if clients are not honest with me. Your attorneys are not here to judge you. We are not here to second-guess your decisions, or to berate you for poor choices. Our job is to take you as you are, dirty laundry and all, assess the facts, and craft a strategy to help you achieve your goals. Yet clients feel the need to withhold critical information from time to time, and let's be clear, when I say, "critical information," I'm not talking about information that the client might not think is relevant. I'm talking about information that the client absolutely knows is relevant, and yet for some reason refuses to disclose to us.

I'm sure that no one in their right mind would insist that their doctor perform surgery with only one hand, or demand that they blindfold themselves while they give you a physical. In the same vein, it's very foolish to ask your lawyer to advocate for you and try and accomplish your goals while refusing to be completely honest and transparent with them.

The truly mind-boggling part of all of this (among others) is that lawyers are generally not cheap. You are paying me to help you. In some cases, you are paying me a large sum of money to help you. Wouldn't you want to give me the best chance and every advantage if I'm fighting for you? Anything that you tell me is protected by the attorney-client privilege, and is therefore confidential. Therefore, it simply makes no sense to withhold information for me, regardless of the reason.

At this point, I should probably chime in with the legal equivalent of a Public Service Announcement: <u>If you don't think I'm going to find out, you're wrong</u>. It will all come out in the end, one way or another. In today's world of public records, computerized asset searches, subpoenas, social media accounts, and a strong tendency amongst the general populace to not keep their mouth shut, your "secret" doesn't have a chance of remaining so. If I catch a client lying to me, or figure out that they are withholding information, I sit them down and give them a lecture (very similar to this chapter, as a matter of fact), and caution them not to do it again. If it happens a second time, they are fired. If I have to find out from opposing counsel that they have been withholding information, or lying about a particular item, they are fired. Being a divorce lawyer is challenging enough without having to deal with this kind of childishness. There are plenty of clients and plenty of other cases I can work on, where people are not determined to shoot themselves in the foot.

Failing to disclose information, or keeping secrets, can only hurt your case. If I find out, it's going to color the relationship between us. I won't know if I can trust you anymore, and that's an untenable position to be in as an attorney. If opposing counsel finds out, he's going to view everything with extreme suspicion. Not only will he doubt what you say, but he might also doubt what I say, since you may very well be lying to me also. If the judge finds out, you have just torpedoed your own case. One of the judge's main functions is to assess the credibility of the parties. If the judge catches you lying, or withholding information, your credibility has just gone out the window (and it's not coming back).

It can also seriously damage your case after the fact. Let's say you get divorced, and six months or a year later it comes out that you withheld information, lied to the court, or failed to disclose something that was relevant. Your wife, or opposing counsel, can file a motion to vacate your divorce judgment and ask the court to throw it away and reopen the case. Not only will this cost you an extreme amount of money, but you will be behind the eight ball for the remainder of the process. In simpler terms, not only will you have to spend more money to essentially litigate the divorce all over again, but now you get to do so in an environment where the judge thinks you have zero credibility. But wait, there could be an even worse outcome. If it becomes apparent to the court that your mistake was not merely an omission, but was deliberate in nature, they can refer your case to the district attorney's or states attorney's office in your jurisdiction, and ask that the prosecutor investigate you for perjury. So now you might have a criminal proceeding hanging over your head, on top of relitigating the divorce. Fraud has consequences, and those consequences are always worse than the situations that honesty creates. In summary, my advice to you is the same advice that has been passed down repeatedly from generation to generation, from the Bible to Ben Franklin: be honest.

MISTAKE #10:
HIRING A 'PITBULL' ATTORNEY, OR, DECIDING ON THE 'SCORCHED EARTH' APPROACH

A long time ago, I had a client that needed to hear a specific message. One day, as we were walking out of court for the fifth time in three weeks, I told him, "You know, in the office we refer to you as the 'boat client'." He looked at me and asked me why that was. I turned to him and told him, in a very sincere manner, "Because if you keep fighting over every single little thing in this case, you'll wind up paying us enough money to go buy a boat." He looked at me and scowled. He didn't like that very much, which was the whole point of me saying it in the first place. Many clients, particularly those who have had to fight their way to the top in their respective professions, can't grasp the concept of running their divorce any other way. They go out and they find an attorney who bills themselves as a "Pitbull", or a "bulldog", or who advertises in such a way to suggest that they will bury your spouse in court. Unfortunately, there are plenty of attorneys who choose to portray themselves in this manner.

In the past 20 to 30 years, the legal profession has seen a rise in the number of firms who advertise themselves as extremely aggressive. Nowhere is this more apparent than with law firms who portray themselves as "fighting for father's rights" or, "defending wives and mothers everywhere." While it's true that specialization is the trend in legal services, what buzzwords and cliché slogans like these really indicate is that these firms will likely use an obscene amount of your money at the beginning of the case, and then withdraw from your case once you are completely out of funds.

This begs the question as to the value of being aggressive in the first place. Now, that may sound like an odd statement to you. I mean, who wants an attorney who's <u>not</u> going to be aggressive? But understand that the term "aggressive" has undergone a transformation in the past 20 to 30 years. The definition of aggression is, "hostile or violent behavior or attitudes towards another," or, "the action or an act of attacking without provocation," or, "forceful and sometimes overly assertive pursuit of one's aims and interests," depending on which dictionary you use. This is an all too accurate description of what goes on during a divorce – <u>between the parties</u>. This is not something that should be going on between the attorneys. "Aggressive" does not mean competent. "Aggressive" does not mean good. "Aggressive" does not mean effective. But over the years this term has somehow acquired those connotations.

Occasionally clients will get upset with an attorney, because they feel that the attorney is not empathizing with them and their situation. In this situation, the client is exactly right. We do not <u>empathize</u> with our clients. We <u>sympathize</u> with our clients and their situation, but we cannot get sucked in to the storm of emotions and the chaotic feelings that accompany so many divorces. Someone in this process must keep a level head and keep their wits about them, and that's us, the attorneys.

That's what you are paying us for. If you're looking for someone to sit there in the courtroom and cry along with you, or give you a hug and validate your feelings, then I suggest you bring a family member or a mental health professional with you. As your legal advocate, we must maintain emotional distance so that we can effectively argue the law and the facts in your case. Crying, hysterics in the courtroom, and emotions that careen wildly from minute to minute are not effective strategies to accomplish your goals. Likewise, indulging in and giving form to your anger and hatred toward your spouse is also not an effective strategy to accomplish your goals. Overly aggressive attorneys, and litigants who decide to "take no prisoners" are not doing anyone a service. Aggression for aggression's sake is not only a poor choice, but it's always more expensive.

Some attorneys cultivate the clients' anger and hatred for their spouses. This serves to pad the attorney's bottom line. Some attorneys have made whole careers out of playing on clients' anger in order to treat the client like an ATM. If a client is furious enough to lash out in the legal system, then they are generally furious enough to pay whatever it takes to do so, even if it is everything they have. Over-lawyering has become an epidemic in the American legal system, and particularly in domestic relations cases. Some attorneys ignore the "counselor" function in their job description, and instead indulge every ill-advised whim and poorly chosen decision that their clients suggest they pursue. This is unfortunate, and thankfully the attorneys that practice this way are few.

The vast majority of attorneys are honest, ethical, and only want what's best for their clients. In fact, I think that most people would be surprised at how often divorce attorneys try to talk their clients out of doing things. Whether it's attempting to convince their client not to spend $3,000 fighting over $1,000, or persuading their client not to violate a court order because they want to give their soon-to-be ex-spouse "a taste of their own medicine", much of what divorce attorneys do is persuading their clients to act in their own best interests, regardless of how the clients "feel" at the moment.

There's a well-known concept in the technology and software industry that goes like this: "If you're not paying for it, then you are the product." This is meant to highlight the fact that, if you are using a 'free' service, the business must be making its money from selling your information to advertisers. There is a similar concept in the divorce process: "If it's about 'the principle', then get your checkbook ready." This highlights the fact that, if your litigation strategy and choices are going to be based on perceived wrongs and various notions of what's "fair", rather than on rational thought, simple math, or good business decisions, then you are going to be dispensing a lot of money into your attorney's pockets.

This "scorched earth" approach leads to wildly escalating costs, without any objective benefit to the client. Granted, there are some scenarios in which an attorney must act quickly and decisively, particularly in scenarios involving the children's well-being. However, most cases never require these sorts of maneuvers. If your attorney is a

"Pitbull", then they will treat every issue as an emergency, and you can plan on being in court very frequently, whether the issues in your case truly require it or not.

Additionally, if your attorney practices in this fashion, then your wife's attorney is going to have to respond in that fashion as well. If your attorney is filing motion after motion after motion, your wife's attorney can't simply ignore those. Your wife's attorney will be filing response after response after response. This ensures that both party's legal bills start to skyrocket. If your wife is a homemaker, or earns significantly less than you do, take a guess on who is going to wind up paying her attorney's bills. That's right, you are, or at least a significant portion of them.

This is one reason that selecting your divorce attorney is so important. In most cities, even large cities, the domestic relations portion of the local bar association is fairly small. This means that most of the attorneys have been practicing, and have known each other, for years. In a lot of cases, if a minor issue comes up, it's a simple thing to pick up the phone and call the other attorney to see if you can't work out a resolution over the phone. This helps the case to run quickly and efficiently, and also dramatically reduces litigation costs. However, if you have chosen an attorney who practices a "take no prisoners" approach, there will be no phone call, email, or letter. There will simply be a motion filed, to which the other side must respond, and which will require at least two trips to the courthouse to resolve. This is how a $500 problem turns into a $3,500 problem.

I mentioned earlier that divorce attorneys spend a lot of time talking their clients out of doing things. One of the examples I used in that context is something that happens very frequently. Very often, the cost of pursuing something in court far exceeds the value of any benefit that will likely be obtained. This is the classical "spending $3,000 to fight over $1,000" scenario. The clients' pride sometimes plays a part in this analysis, where the client feels "wronged" and is determined to battle their spouse. To be honest, the client isn't always wrong. People do frequently behave poorly during a divorce, and they do things they are not supposed to do. Sometimes they are in violation of a court order, or not living up to an agreement that was entered at court. But to some extent, this misses the point. Like the scenario outlined above, do you want to be "right", or do you want to have an extra $2,000 in your pocket?

Avoid disproportionate responses. Just like you wouldn't shoot someone in the face for hitting you with a spit wad, don't do something that negatively impacts you financially just to "prove a point." Some attorneys refer to "fair" as a four-letter word, because it means wildly different things to different people. So rather than focusing on what's "fair", it's usually more helpful to focus on what puts the client in the best position going forward. In this way, you don't let the other side's poor behavior drag you down, financially or otherwise, and you can better preserve your position for the long run.

There are other reasons it pays not to use the "scorched earth" approach. If you and your wife have children, you and your soon-to-be ex must interact and communicate with each other for many years after the divorce is over. There will be birthdays, graduations, and other milestones for which the children will want you there. If your divorce was a bloodbath, this only increases the likelihood that you and your ex will not be able to communicate effectively in areas dealing with the children, and may not be able to peacefully coexist in the same room, even years after the divorce has ended. In extreme cases, you may find yourself not invited, or otherwise unwelcome, at some of your children's milestone events. Although this may be hard to believe, I can think of several instances in which the children don't think of their father as "dad", so much as, "that bastard who put mom through hell", and want nothing to do with him for years after the divorce is final (and in some cases, ever).

People have a hard time forgetting instances of extremely poor behavior, particularly when these instances occur during their childhood. You don't want to do something that will color the relationship between you and your children for the rest of your lives. If wasting all your funds on a "take no prisoners" approach doesn't dissuade you from that course of action, then please, please at least consider the possible impact on your children before you go down that road.

CONCLUSION

When you first saw this book, you probably had some questions immediately spring to mind. Does anybody really "win" in a divorce? Is it even realistic to think you, as a man, can come out ahead in your own divorce? How is that even possible? Isn't the court system stacked against me from the start?

The good news is that things have gotten much, much better for men in our legal system. The statutes and laws and attitudes towards men have gotten much less one-sided in the past ten years. Men still need to be careful that they don't accidentally (or sometimes intentionally) undermine their own efforts and those of their attorney in a divorce, but the system is much fairer these days.

Having reached the end of this book, many of you will note that some of the topics discussed appear to be common sense. Unfortunately, in the emotional turmoil and hurt of the divorce process, much of what we think of as common sense goes out the window. I sometimes feel that there should be a class that every man is required to take, prior to filing for divorce. In this class, I could pound on a podium and reiterate repeatedly what not to do.

But that's not how our world works. My gift to you, and the best information I can give you, is contained in the pages of this book. Whether you're just beginning your divorce journey, or whether you're embroiled in the thick of it, these pages contain a manual for navigating the process without falling victim to the most common pitfalls.

Of course, it's a fair question whether any man can ever truly win their divorce. If you read this book carefully and follow the suggestions in each chapter, you will avoid 99% of the problems men deal with during their divorce. So, go out there, hold your head high, keep your chin up, and prepare to enter the next phase of your life. If you can successfully emerge from your divorce, relatively unscathed, not having suffered due to poor choices and questionable strategy, I think anyone would consider that a win.

ACKNOWLEDGMENTS AND THANKS

Writing a book is always a team effort, even when some people aren't aware that they are on the team. I would like to thank the following people and places for directly (and indirectly) making this book possible:

Chandler Bolt

Jen Sincero

Starbucks (Naperville, IL)

Community Coffee (New Orleans, LA)

Fritzel's Jazz Emporium (New Orleans, LA)

Humidor Cigar Lounge (Westmont, IL)

The Bourbon Orleans Hotel (New Orleans, LA)

Michelle Wulf, editor extraordinaire

C5 Designs

Jennifer Janes

Rudy Ristich

Eric Waltmire

Ken Packard

Peter Thiel

My brothers and sisters in Phi Alpha Delta Law Fraternity, International.

Joseph F. Emmerth

All my colleagues at Sullivan Taylor & Gumina, P.C.

Thank you, for everything.

SHAMELESS REVIEW PLUG PAGE!

If you liked this book, please head over to Amazon.com and leave a review! You and your review are so important to small and independent authors like me. A few reviews can mean the difference between someone (who could really benefit from this book) seeing it or not. Please leave a review and give me any feedback you have! Thank you in advance!

Joseph F. Emmerth

ABOUT THE AUTHOR

JOSEPH F. EMMERTH is a divorce attorney, speaker and author based in Naperville, Illinois. In over a decade of practice, Joseph has helped hundreds of men (and women) successfully navigate their divorce and begin their new lives. He has been voted an Illinois SuperLawyer by his peers since 2012, and was voted the prestigious Avvo Client's Choice Award in 2014. Joseph was appointed to, and still serves on, the Illinois State Bar Association's standing committee on judicial evaluations in 2010, having twice served as Chair of that committee. In his spare time, he enjoys traveling, good cigars, good bourbon, and good conversation. If you need divorce help, or are thinking about getting a divorce, find him online at: www.stglawfirm.com

Made in the USA
Coppell, TX
08 January 2020

14267353R00061